Caves and Mines

Jamie Holloway

Rosen
Classroom™
New York

T0020397

This is a cave. It is a deep hole in the ground. Caves are formed naturally.

A cavern is another name for a cave.

They can be very deep underground.

Caves can also be underwater.

Most caves are created by water dissolving rock. Limestone is a type of rock dissolved by water. This creates beautiful formations.

Caves were used as shelter by early humans. They left many signs of their lives inside caves.

Exploring caves is called caving. It can also be called spelunking.

This is a mine. It is a deep hole dug by people. It is not made naturally.

A mine is used to remove materials. This is called mining. Metal, oil, and stone are some materials found in mines.

Engineers and scientists use math and science to build machines. Machines help engineers remove earth and rock near the surface. Large drills are used to reach materials deep underground.

Diamonds are collected from mines. Gold is also mined. They are both used in jewelry.

Mining began a very long time ago. Flint is a material that was mined. It was used to make arrowheads. Arrowheads were used for protection and hunting.

Glossary

cave   A deep hole in the ground that is formed naturally.

flint   A hard grey mineral used in ancient times to form tools and weapons.

mine   A deep hole in the ground that is dug by people.

mining   The process of removing natural materials from a mine.